REDUCING, REUSING, AND RECYCLING

Bobbie Kalman

The Crabtree Environment Series

 CRABTREE PUBLISHING COMPANY

Created by Bobbie Kalman

For my soul mates Sam and Elvira Graci

Writing team
Bobbie Kalman
Janine Schaub

Editors
Claudia Forgas
Selina Appleby
Peter Crabtree

Computer Layout
Suzanne Jensen

Mechanicals
David Willis
Diane Coderre

Color Separations
Systems Color

Printer
Lake Book Manufacturing

A very special thanks to the teachers and students of Hoover Elementary School, Claudia Forgas, Suzanne Jensen, Samantha Crabtree, Sarah Giesbrecht, Mora and Amber Meyer, Barney Bajardi, and Jocelyn Pepe.

Published by
Crabtree Publishing Company

1110 Kamato Road	350 Fifth Avenue	73 Lime Walk
Unit 4	Suite 3308	Headington
Mississauga, Ontario	New York	Oxford OX3 7AD
Canada L4W 2P3	N.Y. 10118	United Kingdom

Cataloguing in Publication Data

Kalman, Bobbie, 1947-
  Reducing, reusing, and recycling

(The Crabtree environment series)
Includes index.
ISBN 0-86505-426-6 (bound) ISBN 0-86505-456-8 (pbk.)

1. Recycling (Waste, etc.) - Juvenile literature.
2. Salvage (Waste, etc) - Juvenile literature.
I. Title. II. Series: Kalman, Bobbie, 1947- .
The Crabtree environment series.

TD794.5.K35 1991   j 363.72'82

Contents

Earth is our only home!

Not long ago the air, water, and land were clean.

Earth is a perfect planet! It is the only planet in our solar system that supports life—plants, animals, and human beings. People have inhabited the earth for over a million years!

Living naturally

Not very long ago the people of the earth enjoyed clean air, clean water, and a vast, wild landscape. They lived in harmony with nature. They wove their clothes from the wool of sheep and the fibers of plants such as flax and cotton. They carved furniture and tools out of wood. They used vegetable skins, flowers, roots, and herbs to make medicines, dyes, and preservatives.

Before steam power and electricity were invented, almost everything was made by hand. People treasured their few belongings. They recycled their worn-out clothes and tools to make other things from them. For example, sweaters were ripped apart, and the wool was used over again. The little bit of garbage that was thrown out was **biodegradable**. Biodegradable substances break down easily and become part of the earth again.

A new way of life

In just over a hundred years, the lives of people have changed dramatically. Most of us live in cities and buy factory-made goods instead of making the things we need in our homes. Our food, clothes, furniture, and tools are all mass-produced. Most of the things we buy are made from synthetic rather than natural ingredients.

This picture shows how nature is damaged by the garbage people have dumped on the land.

A throwaway society

Because it is so easy to buy the things we want, we do not think twice about throwing away what we no longer need. Unfortunately, most of the objects we discard are made from materials that are indestructible; they will not be absorbed by the earth for thousands of years. Our garbage is also loaded with dangerous chemicals that threaten both wildlife and human life.

We are part of the natural world

For a long time we have not worried about how our thoughtless actions could harm the natural world. But the time has come to realize that our actions towards the environment involve us directly. The poisonous garbage we dump onto the land and into the water and the fumes we release into the atmosphere all enter our bodies through the food we eat, the water we drink, and the air we breathe. Not only are we destroying the environment, we are making ourselves sick!

No time to waste!

In order to reverse the damage we have done, we must learn to care about our environment. As we develop this caring attitude, our actions will no longer be a threat to the natural world. But we have to work together to decrease the amount of pollution and waste we are creating at home, at school, and in our community every single day! We must remember that Earth is our only home. It is the duty of each one of us to help save our planet. There is no more time to waste!

The three Rs

People who are concerned about the environment are working hard to clean up the earth by practicing three simple techniques known as the three Rs. The three Rs of waste management are always listed in the order that they should be followed: **reduction** is first, **reuse** second, and **recycling** third. In this book we will use the terms reducing, reusing, and recycling because the "ing" endings suggest that our efforts and actions are active and ongoing.

By practicing the three Rs, we can cut down on the amount of raw materials we use and the volume of garbage we create. The result will be a cleaner, healthier planet.

Reducing our garbage

Reducing is the most important of the three Rs. It means creating a lot less garbage! Reducing is also the most difficult of the three Rs because it requires much thought and self-sacrifice.

Changing our wasteful habits

We have to think about our daily wasteful habits such as using paper products that need to be thrown away instead of cloth ones that can be washed and reused. When we shop, we should ask ourselves, "Do I really need this?" We could also consider whether the things we buy will create garbage. Do they have too much packaging? Will they go out of fashion quickly? Changing our wasteful habits requires a lot of self discipline!

Using cloth instead of paper helps reduce garbage.

Saving the earth's resources

If people reduce the number and types of goods they purchase, fewer goods will need to be manufactured, and fewer natural resources will be used. For instance, if we buy unwrapped products, we will save trees and oil from which packaging is made.

What can you do?

You may not be the one who decides what is purchased in your household, but your parents probably buy a lot of things for you. You can reduce the purchases your family makes by asking for less. Do you really need another jacket? Can you borrow video games from a video-rental store instead of buying them?

Waste not, want not!

Besides cutting back on your buying, you can also practice garbage reduction by not wasting things. Do you take three tissues when using one would be sufficient? Do you buy magazines and throw them away after you have read them? There are many ideas and activities in this book to help you reduce the amount of garbage you create. Make them part of your everyday routine.

There is so much garbage that almost every landfill on earth is now or, will soon be, full.

Set a goal

You and your family can set a goal to reduce your garbage a little each week. If you put out three big bags of trash now, try reducing your rubbish to two-and-a-half bags. Next week you can make two bags your goal, and then one bag, and so on. With the help of reusing and recycling practices, you can really cut down on your garbage in a very short time.

Using the three Rs, you can reduce your garbage from a big bag to a small one, as Barney has.

Reusing helps reduce garbage

Reusing means saving items that usually would be thrown out and using them over again. When we reuse, we again save natural resources because we need to produce fewer new goods. We save money by not buying new things, and we save space at the landfill site. Reusing goes hand-in-hand with reducing. By reusing, we also reduce the amount we throw out.

Simple ways to reuse

Here are some simple ways you and your friends can reuse things. Remember! You are saving money and natural resources.

- Yarn, material remnants, buttons, egg cartons, toilet-paper tubes, boxes, thread spools, film containers, paper clips, hooks, and fruit baskets can be taken to your school or given to a day-care center for use as art materials.

- When everyone is finished reading the household magazines, give them to a hospital or doctor's waiting room.
- Old eye glasses can be donated to the Institute for the Blind or to third-world organizations, which sort, remodel, and distribute them to needy people.
- If you have clothes that are in good condition but do not fit you anymore, sell them to a second-hand clothing shop or give them to a charitable organization.

Bag brainstorming

With little thought, it is easy to change yourself into a conserving individual. Consider the number of plastic bags you use only once and then throw out. With some bag brainstorming, you can think up all sorts of second- and third-time uses for bags. Here are just a few:

- Take your old bags to the grocery store and reuse them when you go shopping.
- Washed-out milk bags make excellent containers for freezing food. Freezer vegetable bags can be used over again.
- Give away extra bags to a local food bank or to someone who runs his or her own business and needs lots of bags.
- Find out if the supermarkets in your area collect used plastic bags for recycling. Some supermarkets forward plastic bags to recycling centers where the bags are sorted, cleaned, and ground up to make new plastic bags, which can be used over and over again.

School students can use your leftover materials for their art projects.

Better batteries

Do you listen to music while you are walking to a friend's house or to school? Portable cassette and compact disc players use a lot of batteries in a short time! Batteries contain poisonous substances such as mercury and cadmium that can leak out at a landfill and produce dangerous ashes when they are incinerated. Instead of using several batteries a month, invest in a battery charger and some rechargeable batteries. Although the batteries are more expensive to begin with, they will save you money in the long run, and you will help save the environment. If you do have old batteries to throw away, make sure they are saved and disposed of at a hazardous-waste collection.

Garage sales and flea markets

Garage sales and flea markets are based on the idea that one person's trash is another's treasure. Instead of throwing out your still-useful old belongings, plan a sale with some of your friends. With a parent's permission collect a variety of toys, books, and household items that you think someone else might be interested in buying. Be sure to plan your sale in advance, advertise it, and consider what you are going to do with the leftovers. You may want to donate the money that you have made to a local food bank or to a community clean-up project.

Fix it!

Instead of taking the time and effort to repair things, many people just throw them out. The next time someone in your family is about to discard something, check if it could be mended, refinished, or remodeled.

Exchanging old games can bring new fun!

"Save-it" room

Turn an unused room or closet in your school into a place to store discarded but potentially useful materials. Develop a system for organizing the collected materials and keeping them tidy. When students from your school are planning a project, they could visit the "save-it" room instead of using new materials. If the idea really catches on, an award could be given for the most unique use of saved materials.

The great exchange

Could you trade something of yours for another used item? Set up a trading center at your school. You could operate it as a lending library or a place to make exchanges. Exchanging is great way of getting rid of old games, toys, and clothes and replacing them with ones that are new to you. You may find some very interesting treasures! You will also save some of your allowance and cut down on your garbage.

Recycling natural resources

Most of the garbage we throw out was made from valuable natural resources such as trees and oil. Through recycling we can reuse many of these natural resources by turning them into new products. Glass can be ground up and made into new bottles, and tins can be manufactured into new cans. Newspapers can be deinked to produce new newsprint and lightweight cardboard boxes. Recycling is a great way to reduce our garbage and save natural resources. For example, recycling paper saves cutting down millions of trees.

Newspaper recycling

Newspapers are separated from the other recyclables and sent to a paper mill to be deinked. Using special soaps, the paper is churned into pulp and passed through a series of filters to remove chemicals. The cleaned pulp is mixed with new pulp and is rolled into paper to make newsprint, box board, and building materials such as ceiling tiles and insulation.

Steel and aluminum cans

In a recycling plant the steel cans are separated from the lighter aluminum cans by a magnetic separator. Then they are cleaned and "detinned." The protective tin layer they contain is removed in this process. The detinned cans are fed into steel-making furnaces. The steel is reused to make new cans and many other household products and appliances.

Aluminum cans are first shredded and then stripped of their lacquer. Lacquer is the material that makes them shiny and protects their surface. After the delacquering process, the cans are melted down into aluminum sheets to make products such as new soft-drink cans.

What happens to glass?

Glass bottles and jars are reduced to **cullet**, which is crushed glass. The cullet is mixed with sand, limestone, and soda ash and then melted in high-temperature furnaces. The melted or "molten" glass is shaped into new containers. Recycled glass is also used to make construction materials.

Plastic bottles and jugs

Presently only a few types of plastic can be recycled. Plastic containers often contain many layers of different kinds of plastic that are difficult to separate. Soft-drink bottles made from a thin, clear plastic called **polyethylene terephthalate** (PET) are recyclable. They are sorted and ground into flakes and then into pellets, which are used to fill ski jackets and sleeping bags. Drain pipes, plastic bags, and household appliances are also made from the pellets.

Fine-paper recycling

Schools and businesses use a lot of white paper every day for letters and computer printouts. Until recently this paper ended up at the landfill site. Fortunately, many institutions are now taking part in fine-paper recycling. Fine paper, such as that used by you and your friends each day, is collected, made into pulp again, and then manufactured into tissue, writing paper, and newsprint. Does your school recycle its fine paper? It should!

The Mobius Loop

The well-known symbol shown below is used by recycling groups and industries throughout North America and Europe. If a product is stamped with the Mobius Loop, it is either produced from recycled materials or is recyclable. The symbol shows the never-ending use and reuse of materials. One arrow goes into another, just as materials get recycled into new products to be used over and over again.

The Mobius Loop

source separation

buying
recycled
products

breaking down
recyclables

manufacturing
recycled goods

Completing the cycle

As you can see, recycling is not just putting cans and bottles into the blue box. This part, called **source separation**, is followed by a process of breaking down the recyclables, manufacturing new products from them, and then selling the recycled products. To make recycling work, the process must come full circle. We not only have to collect recyclable materials, we must also make sure that new goods are produced from these materials. When people buy goods made from recycled materials, they are helping the cause of recycling. The more recycled goods bought, such as computer paper, the more demand there will be for products made from recycled materials.

Cans and bottles can be recycled to make new products.

Aluminum cans are compacted into huge cubes and sent to be shredded.

Fine paper is shredded and made into new pulp.

11

How to participate

Many communities have provided every household with a blue box for collecting recyclable goods. In most places newspapers, glass bottles and jars, tin cans, and some plastics can be recycled.

As the week goes by, fill up your box. Make sure you rinse out all food particles and remove screw tops from bottles. Every one or two weeks a recycling truck will come to pick up the materials you leave by the curb in your box. In some areas curbside programs are not yet set up. If you live in one of these communities, you and your parents can locate the nearest depot where you can drop off your carefully collected recyclable materials. These depots are often located in supermarket parking lots.

Why recycle?
- Recycling reduces garbage. Every item that goes into the recycling bin is one less item in a landfill site.
- Recycling conserves natural resources.
- Recycling saves energy. It takes far less energy to produce goods from recycled metal, glass, and paper than from raw materials. For example, it takes 70 percent less energy to produce aluminum from recycled products. Because recycled objects take less energy to make, factories create less air and water pollution.
- Recycling creates jobs. Thousands of new jobs could be created by increasing the number of recycling programs and businesses that involve recycling.

Overeager recyclers

In many communities recycling programs have caught on like wild fire. People are eager to do what they can to save the environment. Unfortunately, a few people are overeager. Instead of being careful to put only recyclable items into their blue boxes, some individuals include anything they need to throw out. Old toasters, broken chinaware, window glass, glossy magazines, and worn-out rubber boots all end up in the recycling bin, although they cannot yet be recycled. By including these things in your box, you are creating problems both for the people who collect the contents of the blue boxes and for the workers at the recycling plant because the unwanted objects must be sorted out from the recyclable materials. The objects that cannot be recycled must then be disposed of at a landfill site or incineration plant.

Not the only way!

Recycling makes us feel good because it shows that we are doing something positive for the environment. Of the three Rs, it is the easiest "R" to accomplish. Although recycling is an important way of reducing our garbage, we should not think that filling our blue boxes is all we have to do. We must strive hard to cut down on what we throw out by not creating garbage in the first place!

Recycling resources

Do some research and make a list of all the different companies that reuse and recycle waste in your community. What kinds of waste do these companies handle? Where do they get rid of materials that they cannot use? Design a pamphlet containing the information you find and donate it to the school library as a resource.

The recyclables you put into your blue box are taken to a recycling depot, where they are sorted, compacted, and bundled. After this process the different items are broken down and made into new products for you to buy.

Become a careful consumer

One of the reasons that we have so much garbage on earth is that we are part of a **consumer society**. Consumers are people who buy things. Consumers also throw many things away. Careful consumers, who care about reducing the amount of garbage they create, use good judgement to make thoughtful buying decisions. They avoid buying things that are harmful to the environment.

Even if you are not directly responsible for purchasing many of the things in your home, your opinion counts. You can educate your family to shop more wisely.

Consider the garbage

Before buying, consider the amount of pollution and waste that were created in the manufacture of the products you intend to purchase. Think about how much garbage will be left after you are finished using these products. Disposable items such as throwaway plates and napkins and convenience goods such as canned whipped cream are examples of waste-producing products.

Buy quality

Quality items cost more to begin with, but they save money in the end because they last longer and need fewer repairs. Shop around and compare before choosing the product you intent to buy. Ask the sales clerk which version of the product has the best performance record or find out about the product in a consumer's guide. Do not buy products that are designed to be outdated in a short time.

Check packaging

Many items have unnecessary packaging that is used to advertise the product. In most cases equally good products are available with less plastic and cardboard around them. Although the package may look attractive to you, remember that it is really garbage. Once you take out the toy or game, that attractive package becomes just a piece of trash!

- Choose items in recycled packages.
- Avoid items that hang on racks in bubble packs. Instead, buy items such as unpackaged stationery, pens, and writing pads from bulk bins or shelves.
- Buy unwrapped fruit and vegetables.
- Buy eggs in cardboard cartons instead of Styrofoam ones.
- Choose items that are sold in large containers. Two small boxes of cereal create more garbage than one larger box.
- Avoid snack items that are sold in single-serving containers.
- Take your own baskets or cloth shopping bags to the supermarket. Do not take a bag if you have only one or two items.

Refill, recycle, and rebuy

Buy jars, bottles, and other containers that are returnable or refillable, or choose containers that are recyclable. Many items such as soft-drink containers are now marked with the Mobius Loop to indicate that they can be recycled. To complete the cycle, support businesses that create recycled products by "rebuying" products that were once other products.

A shopping checklist

Next time you go grocery shopping with your parents, try this experiment. Every time you put an item into the cart, ask yourself the following questions:

- Does this item have unnecessary packaging?
- Can its container be reused or recycled?
- Could I buy a similar item with less packaging?
- Is this product going to endanger the environment when I throw it away?
- What pollution and wastes were created when this product was manufactured?
- Is the product recycled?

If you find that your family is choosing too many over-packaged, non-recyclable, and potentially dangerous items, you should definitely take steps to change your purchasing habits. Careful consumers throw out less garbage and less dangerous waste than people who do not think about what they buy and throw away.

Where do you shop?

Is your supermarket concerned about ecology? Does it use recycled paper in its advertising flyers? Do its shopping bags contain recycled plastic? Does it offer a variety of "green" products? Does it encourage its suppliers to reduce packaging? Does it sell unwrapped produce? If not, suggest some changes to the store manager. If your efforts fail, it is time to shop at another supermarket!

(top) Buy unwrapped fruits and vegetables! (middle) Most stores carry unbleached recycled paper products. (bottom) Does your supermarket sell "green" products?

15

Developing a new attitude

We can become active participants in the campaign to save the environment by changing the way we feel about the world. We can develop a new attitude if we are aware of the consequences of everything we do. This is not always easy, but it will make us feel good because we are doing something positive to save our world.

Change takes effort

Change is hard for everyone. Your parents may not want to listen to your new ideas or might be too busy to get involved in ecology issues. It is up to you to encourage your family by setting a good example. For instance, if you want your family to get involved with the recycling program in your community, offer to take the recycling bin to the curb every week. For birthdays and other gift-giving occasions, you can buy environmentally friendly gifts. A cloth shopping bag or a book on organic gardening may start your mother or father down the healthy-environment path.

Positive reminders

Our thoughtless actions towards the environment harm us. We must learn to be responsible, caring human beings who think peaceful, positive thoughts. By changing the way we think and act, we can influence others to do likewise.

A good way to remind yourself of your mission is to write one positive ideal or "affirmation" on a piece of paper each day and carry it in your pocket. Glance at the affirmation several times a day to remind yourself to act responsibly toward the environment. It is best to write your own affirmations. Use positive words, and write your affirmations in the present tense. These examples can get you started.

- I am a considerate, caring person.
- I am a part of nature, and nature is a part of me.
- My world is healthy and clean.
- I am in harmony with my world.
- Each day I am cutting down on the waste I produce.
- I have the power to heal my planet.
- I am one with all life on earth.

No matter how simple or complicated, affirmations can make a difference in the way you think and act. You will soon notice positive changes in your behavior.

Writing affirmations and reading them throughout the day will help you develop a new attitude about your relationship with the natural world.

Imagine!

Close your eyes. Imagine a huge landfill full of trash. What do you see? Are there newspapers, cans, and bottles that could have been recycled? Can you spot some clothes that might have been given to a charity or a bicycle that could have been fixed? Are there food scraps that should have been composted?

Pretend you can move each item in the landfill with your mind. Place all cans, bottles, and newspapers into a huge recycling box. Put books, games, toys, and clothing into a church bazaar and food scraps into a compost bin. Before long, you will have reduced your landfill to a small pile of trash.

By visualizing the things we should reuse and recycle, we will train ourselves to put these objects in their proper places. We will think about what we throw away each day and realize that we have the power to clean up the world.

"Save-the-environment" book

People all over the country are working hard to clean up the environment. Some are planting trees; others are busy trying to convince politicians to change laws. Groups of students are picking up litter in parks and along beaches.

To record the accomplishments of you and your friends, start a "save-the-environment" book at your school. Each time you or another student has done something positive about reducing garbage or saving natural resources, write it down in the book. Writing down your ecological victories, no matter how small, will make you feel good and will surely inspire more environmentally friendly deeds!

Imagine there's no garbage!

Earth Day every day

Earth Day is a yearly celebration. In every country people gather to clean up litter, plant more than a billion trees, and spread information about ways to save the earth. On this day everyone is very excited about doing his or her part. Unfortunately, for many people, caring about the environment is a one-day event. If we want to clean up our world, we must keep the spirit of Earth Day alive every day of the year!

Even young children help pick up litter.

"I will treat the earth kindly."

Samantha reads the suggested ecology pledges and then makes a committment to reduce her garbage.

"I pledge to save the earth!"

During Earth Day you probably made a pledge to do a number of things that would save natural resources and help clean up the earth. Have you kept your promise? Here is a list of some sample Earth Day pledges. Which ones have **you** put into practice?

- I will make a conscious effort to reduce my garbage this year.
- I will trade, lend, and borrow whenever possible to avoid buying something I do not need.
- I will pick up litter when I see it.
- I will recycle cans, bottles, and papers.
- I will put all my used note paper into the fine-paper recycling bin.
- I will take my lunch to school in a reusable plastic container and my juice in a thermos. I will compost my leftover food.
- I will take the recycling bin to the curb each week.
- I will not buy products that are harmful to the environment.

Only one Earth!

The Wholearth Ball shown above was created using NASA photographs, weather-satellite pictures, and maps to portray Earth as it would look from space. Notice that this model of our planet contains no country names or boundaries. By looking at Earth as we would view it from space, we get a real sense that Earth is one planet—the only one on which we can live.

The Wholearth Ball can help you get a feeling for the "oneness" of our world. Hold it in your hands. Marvel at the beauty of the planet by noticing the colors of the oceans, forests, and deserts. Let your gaze follow the cloud formations. Visualize yourself as a tiny speck on the surface of the earth. Imagine the floating sensation of weightlessness that you would experience if you were viewing Earth from space.

Sense your physical connection to nature. Understand that people, plants, and animals depend on one another. Acknowledge the limitless kindness of nature's gifts to humankind. Thank the earth for nourishing you. Appreciate it for being your home. There is only one Earth. Will you help care for it?

Appreciate your natural world

Take a leisurely walk in your neighborhood and spend some time looking at all the natural wonders along the way. Do you know the names of the animals and plants that live around you? Have you ever read a story or researched facts about your local environment? Go to the library and find all the information you can. Once you learn about the living things that share your world, you will feel much more connected to nature.

Good food sense

Much of our garbage is related to food. Did you know that almost a quarter of the food that most families buy ends up in the trash? Another source of waste is the packaging in which we buy food. Most food comes wrapped in unnecessary bags and boxes. Here are some simple ways you can make better choices about the food you eat. The end result could be a lot less garbage.

Eat real foods

Learn to appreciate foods that look like real food rather that powdered, packaged, and canned versions. Real potatoes are better for you than potato chips. Try eating more fresh foods and less processed foods. Next time you reach for food in a box or can, read the list of ingredients. Notice the sugar, salt, and preservatives. These additives are not good for your health!

Eat real foods such as these.

We do not need to eat meat at every meal. Eating more vegetables and grain products than meat conserves valuable natural resources. Raising cattle, sheep, pigs, and chickens to supply people with meat uses up huge areas of land, an enormous amount of grain, and a lot of fresh water.

Start a vegetable and herb garden

If you have a back yard, convince your parents to help you plant some vegetables. Tomatoes, cucumbers, zucchini, green peppers, and radishes are all easy to grow and much more delicious to eat when they are fresh. Experiment with some herbs, too. Mint, basil, parsley, oregano, and tarragon will make your food taste delicious. You will learn to appreciate food in a brand-new way by adding these herbs to your salads, sandwiches, dips, and drinks. Using your fresh vegetables and herbs, try these recipes and then make up your own.

Pita snack

Chop up some zucchini, tomato, and onion and fill one half of a pita bread with these vegetables. Grate some cheese and sprinkle it into the pita pocket. Microwave your pita snack on high for one to two minutes. Add a handful of fresh chopped parsley or basil. Enjoy your healthy and delicious snack!

Refreshing mint drinks

Here are some refreshing drinks you can make with mint from your garden:

To a glass of cranberry, raspberry, or loganberry juice, add ice cubes, a squeeze of lime, and a sprig of mint. Try boiling mint in water for hot mint tea, or add ice cubes and drink it cold. Mint helps you digest your food and leaves your mouth tasting fresh.

Lunch time—trash time

Many children take their lunches to school each day. A typical lunch might consist of a sandwich, dessert, a fruit, and a drink.

In recent years food companies have created advertising gimmicks to fool parents and children into buying products that would avoid what the ads call "lunchbag letdown." Advertisers have convinced us that we need to make our lunches more colorful and exciting by including individually packaged snack packs, pudding and fruit cups, drink boxes, and cookies and cup cakes.

All these fancy foods have one thing in common. They all come wrapped in garbage. With each item we eat, we throw away a piece of packaging. We also waste the natural resources that were used to create that packaging.

You can avoid "lunchbag letdown" by discussing your lunchtime preferences with your parents. There are many ways to make your lunch more interesting without having to buy packaged items. Sandwiches, salads, cheese and crackers, and cakes and cookies can all be taken to school in reusable plastic containers. Juice can be brought in a thermos, and a piece of fresh fruit is healthier than canned fruit.

When you use your imagination to prepare lunches you like, you will also throw away less food. There is no need to discard a single piece of garbage at lunchtime. What about your apple core? Take it home and add it to your compost!

Squirmy, slimy natural wonders!

If your family does not have a compost bin or pile, encourage them to start one. Composting is probably one of the most important ways to reduce your garbage.

Worms are super composters!

Whoever thinks worms are just slimy little creatures that come out on rainy days could not be farther from the truth. These tubular critters are great friends of the earth! They are super composters.

Composting with worms is called **vermi-composting**. Vermi-composting can be done by anyone—even those who live in apartments. You don't have to worry that the worms will crawl out of their home and try to become part of your family! Just follow this easy recipe, and you're sure to have a successful "vermi village."

This slimy wonder is nature's little helper.

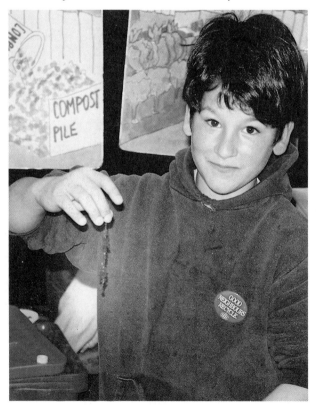

Vermi-village recipe

Ingredients:

- 1 pound (400 grams) red worms
- 1 garbage bin, bucket, old wash tub, or large ceramic pot.
- 1 lid and 1 tray
- Bedding made of a mix of organic material. You can use straw, chopped plants, leaves, and shredded cardboard.

Leftover fruit and vegetables and garden clippings can all be composted.

Your final product, humus, will look like this.

Directions:

- Poke holes in the bottom of your bin. Place the bin on the tray so that water can drain out.
- Put the bedding in the bottom of the bin and dampen it thoroughly.
- Add the worms. Cover with the lid.
- Place your vermi village in a cool, dark place, but make sure the temperature does not go below the freezing point.
- Feed your worms organic wastes such as coffee grinds, vegetable and fruit left-overs, dust balls and egg shells. Do not feed them meats or fatty foods.
- When your compost looks like dark, black soil, it has turned into a nutritious fertilizer called **humus**, and your compost is finished. Use the humus in your garden or, if you do not have one, give it to a friend who has. The worms will find a new home outdoors, and you can start another compost with a new batch of wrigglers.

A song and dance about worms

Write a song about worms. An easy way to write a song is to start with a tune you know and then write words that fit. If you are good at making up music, then hum your original tune into a tape-recorder so you don't forget it. You can tell your story in the body of the song and repeat your main message in the refrain.

Have a group of friends hiss, clap, make mouth noises, and slap their legs to help you keep the beat. Then make up a dance to go with your song. Call it a "squirm" dance!

Will your squirm dance look like this?

Garbage fun

Gift boxes for all occasions

Does your family give gifts wrapped in colorful paper and adorned with shiny ribbons? Is there a mountain of boxes, crumpled papers, and discarded bows on the floor after a birthday party or on Christmas morning?

Most people find themselves in this situation on special gift-giving occasions. You can start a new trend that will cut down on garbage by making several prewrapped gift boxes for birthdays, Mother's and Father's Day, Christmas, Hanukkah, or other gift-giving occasions.

Wrap the tops and bottoms of the boxes separately so that, when put together, the wrapped top fits over the wrapped bottom, and nothing needs to be ripped or thrown out. Decorate the wrapped boxes with bows, cutouts, sequins, or buttons. When you give your friends a present, ask them to reuse the box, or keep it yourself. By not buying new wrapping paper, you will save money and a lot of trees. You will also cut down on bags and bags of garbage!

The garbage game

Design a board game about trash! Different squares on the board could tell the players to pick up violation cards or 3R cards. Violation cards might say, "Did not recycle your bottles and cans—go back to start!" or "Dogs spill your trash can, miss one turn." An example of a 3R card might be, "You compost your food scraps. Move ahead three spaces." The object of the game is to be the first to arrive at the recycling depot. Instead of using cards, you could invent a trivia or word game about the environment. On a rainy day, get yourself out of the "dumps" with some creative garbage fun!

Junk jewelry

You will need the following supplies to make your own junk-jewelry necklace:

- a ribbon or cord long enough to go around your neck
- a piece of felt or velvet
- some old beads
- an assortment of small junk items of your choice, such as buttons, sequins, old earrings, pieces of net, tiny dolls, and miniature toys
- glue, scissors, a needle, and thread

Cut an oval out of the felt or velvet, fold it in half, and sew it together at the edges. Make a hole at both edges so that you can thread a ribbon through. String your old beads on the ribbon. Attach your junk treasures to the felt with glue or sew them on to make an interesting collage, such as the one shown in the top left photograph.

(left) You'll get many compliments on your junk necklace.

(right) Have fun making and playing with your garbage game!

(bottom) These students are modeling their "garbage hats." With them is the author, wearing her junk necklace.

(top) Pulp the papers in a blender. (bottom) Lift the screen straight up, keeping it level. (right) Rolling the screen gently from side to side to dislodge the paper is called **couching off.**

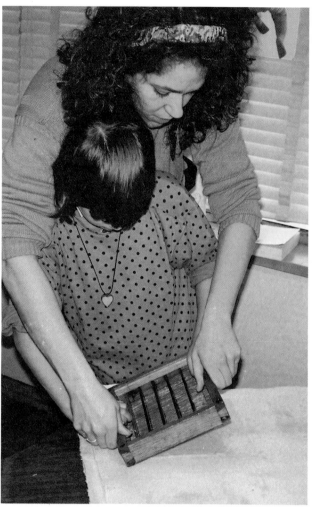

Making recycled paper

To make your own recycled paper, you will need the following supplies:

- scrap white paper
- a blender
- a large tub, pail, or aquarium
- wire mesh stretched on a wooden frame (an old window screen could be used as an alternative)
- newspapers or pieces of absorbent cloth
- a lot of water

Collect sheets of used white paper, junk mail, and envelopes until you have a small pile. Tear the sheets into tiny pieces and put them into a container. Cover the paper with water—one part paper to two parts water.

Let this mixture soak overnight. The next day "pulp" the fibers in the paper by beating the wet paper in a blender. Make sure you have plenty of water in your blender or you will burn out the motor! You may want to add some vegetable peels or flower petals for interesting effects. When done, the mixture should resemble mush.

Fill your tub halfway with water. Dump in the pulp mixture. Grasp your screen with both hands, immerse it into the tub, and shake it gently from side to side. In a single straight motion, lift the screen out of the tub. Water will rush through the mesh, and the paper fiber will coat the screen evenly. Be sure to keep the screen level, or one side of your paper will be thicker than the other. Turn your screen upside-down onto a stack of cloth pieces or newspaper pages by rolling it slowly but steadily from one edge of the screen to another. Your recycled paper will stay on the newspaper or cloth.

Garbage art

When someone says your art is garbage, it may not be an insult! Some of the best art ever created has been made from materials that other people have thrown away. Scrap lumber, watch parts, bits of foil, steel and aluminum cans, and toilet-paper rolls all can be used to construct a marvelous invention, a novel sculpture, or even pieces of jewelry. Ask your neighbors and friends if they have any interesting trash they could give you. Start a bin for the collection of objects that would have been thrown away. Whenever you want to create, look in your bin for inspiration!

(right; top) Express you feelings about nature through body talk. (bottom) Using garbage, you can create interesting art pieces.

Body talk

When a feeling circulates freely inside you and your body responds to it, you have body talk. You can experience your feelings about the earth by stretching your body long and wide, curling it up small, and by shaking your arms, legs, head, and torso gently. Feel what it is like to be the wind, a tree, a lion, a tiny bug, or a butterfly.

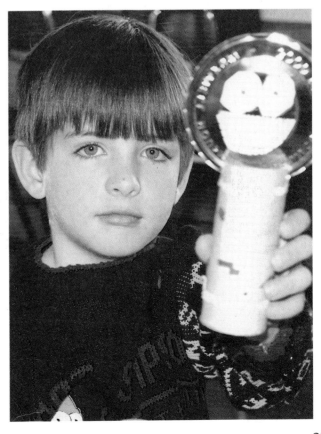

Take action!

The most important way to help people jump on the ecology bandwagon is to give them information. When people become aware of the facts, they will want to do their part. The more they hear about ecology problems, the more the message will sink in. So don't give up—keep gabbing about garbage, and you are sure to get your message across!

A forum on garbage

Collect newspaper articles dealing with recycling and waste disposal. Examine the issues on which the articles focus and use the information to start a "forum on garbage." For example, there might be articles about the construction of a new incineration plant in your area. Your group could find more information on the subject, debate the pros and cons of incineration, and suggest better ways to reduce the garbage in your community. Your school could launch a program promoting household and community composting as an alternative. Ask the newspapers to cover your campaign.

Hazardous-waste poster

Many areas provide collection programs for hazardous wastes. Hazardous wastes are materials that require special handling precautions during disposal to prevent damage to people, property, and the environment. If your community does not have a program set up to dispose of hazardous household wastes, contact your mayor or city councillors and encourage them to get started. Obtain lists of hazardous household materials that should not be thrown out with the regular garbage and distribute the lists in your community. Make up posters explaining what hazardous wastes are and why they need special collection.

The students in the top photograph show concern for the environment by holding a forum on garbage.

Making posters showing the dangers of hazardous wastes is an "earthy" activity.

Make your government work for you

If you have a concern about a garbage issue or about your city's system of waste disposal, write a letter to a local politician. Letter writing can be a very effective way of bringing about change—especially when several people write to the same person concerning the same issue. Politicians are responsible to the public and must take action if the people who elected them want something done. When you write your letter, keep the following points in mind:

- Stick to one subject
- Be specific about the issue
- Ask direct questions such as "What actions does your department plan to take to ensure proper disposal of hazardous household waste?"
- Use local examples to prove your point.
- Be persistent—it may take several letters to get your point across.

The three students shown above are displaying the letters they wrote to their local politician and the reply they received concerning an ecology issue.

Public meetings

Another way your opinion can be heard is by asking your parents to attend public meetings on ecology issues. If your community is opposed to changes that are dangerous to your local environment, you and your neighbors can fight these changes by attending public meetings, where you can let your opinions be heard concerning community projects.

A multi-media environment event

Hold a multi-media environment event in your classroom, or make it a schoolwide celebration. Find as many ways as you can to spread your message. Here are some sample ideas: make up a play, write songs, play recycling games, draw pictures, hold a composting demonstration, design posters and banners, make a garbage sculpture, clean up the school yard, recite speeches, and hold debates. Take videotapes and photographs of garbage-strewn areas in your community and make plans to clean them up.

How big is your waste line?

How much garbage do you throw out? Try this quiz to see if your waste line needs reducing! Score one point for each question to which you answer yes.

- Can you name the three Rs?
- Do you compost your food scraps?
- Do you recycle newspapers, cans, and bottles?
- Do you look for refillable, reusable, and recyclable containers?
- Whenever possible, do you choose to buy goods made from recycled materials?
- Do you avoid over-packaged products?
- Do you use cloths and sponges instead of paper products?
- Do you trade and borrow instead of buying something new?
- Do you shop at garage sales and second-hand stores?
- Do you take garbage-free lunches to school?
- Do you make a habit of repairing things instead of throwing them out and buying new items?
- Do you know where to get rid of hazardous household wastes in your community?

Scores:

10-12: Congratulations! You are doing your part to save the planet!

7-9: You have done some serious thinking and it shows! Keep your waste line trim!

5-8: Do not waste time. Clean up your act before our landfill sites are land**full** sites!

O-4: You need to make a trip to a landfill to inspire you to reduce your waste line.

In which ways have you reduced your waste line?

Pass it on!

Once you learn how to reduce and recycle waste, you can help others get started. All most people need is a little encouragement and some information about how to make the three Rs work for them. Pass on your knowledge concerning waste management and, hopefully, others will pass on theirs, too. By adjusting your lifestyle to include reducing, reusing, and recycling practices, not only can you become part of the solution to today's garbage problem, but you can also set a good example for others to follow. Remember—gab about garbage!

Glossary

additive Something that is added to a product

affirmation A positive statement or declaration

biodegradable A substance that is capable of breaking down into a harmless form

box board A thin type of cardboard used to make small boxes, e.g. cereal boxes

cadmium A white, metallic substance that can cause serious health problems to human beings and animals

collage A picture made by gluing pieces of various materials in a desired pattern

compost A mixture of vegetable matter and other biodegradables that breaks down into fertilizer over a short period

consumer society A society that uses articles made by others

convenience Something that saves time and work and allows more comfort

cullet Crushed glass

depot A storage place

ecology A study of the relationship between living things and their environment

environment The surroundings that affect the existence of living beings

fine-paper recycling The recycling of good-quality paper such as computer paper, letter paper, and white envelopes

hazardous waste Garbage that is dangerous to living beings

hazardous-waste collection A collection point for dangerous garbage

humus A dark soil-like substance that consists of decayed vegetable matter and contains plant nutrients

incineration Burning garbage to ashes

landfill A place where garbage is buried under and on top of layers of dirt

magnetic separator A piece of machinery that uses the power of a magnet to separate certain types of metals from other types

mercury A heavy, shiny, silver-colored, poisonous metallic element

natural resources Materials found in nature that are useful to people or necessary to their survival, such as water, trees, and minerals

packaging A wrapping or container into which something is packed

pita Flat, round bread that originated in the Middle East. It opens like a pocket.

polyethylene terephthalate A clear, thin, plastic used to make soft-drink bottles

processed Made or prepared by some special method

pulp A soft, moist, formless mass, such as the mixture of matted fibers of wood that is used in making paper

raw material Material not yet refined, manufactured, or processed

remnant A piece of cloth left over from the cutting of a larger piece

Styrofoam Lightweight plastic used in making drinking cups, etc. Also known as polystyrene foam

synthetic Not made from natural materials

third world Describing countries that are considered less developed in their industry and social programs

toxic waste Poisonous garbage

vermi-composting Using worms to speed up the disintegration of biodegradable substances

visualization The process of producing an image in the mind

waste management The handling and controlling of garbage

Index & Acknowledgments

Special thanks to: the principal, librarians, students, and teachers of Hoover Elementary School in Kenmore, N. Y., who provided many of the photo opportunities. They are: Michael Giallombardo (principal); John Freda (ecology teacher); Joanne Storer-Giambrone (organiser and librarian); Christina Lucas (art teacher); Toni Sciog, Kathy Shotwell, Nancy Linton, Charlotte Huebschman (classroom teachers); and Becky Camhi (elementary librarian). I would also like to thank DeLaat's Valumart and EarthSource. **Photo credits:** Peter Crabtree and Bobbie Kalman: Cover, title page, 4, 6, 7 (bottom), 8, 9, 12, 15, 16, 18, 19, 20, 22 (taken at "Public Focus" Children's Environment Festival), 23, 25, 26, 27, 28, 29, 30; Courtesy of the Ontario Ministry of the Environment: 7 (top), 11, 13, 17. **Artwork:** Elaine Macpherson: 5; Brenda Clark: 17; Greg Ruhl: 21; Karen Harrison: 24.

1 2 3 4 5 6 7 8 9 Printed in U.S.A. 0 9 8 7 6 5 4 3 2 1